Love Letters from

My Kitchen

Beth Anne Van Horn

Dedication

I dedicate this book to Aidan. My prayer for you is health. No matter how old you get, you will always be my firstborn, my baby. You taught me how a mother's love transforms a heart. Thank you. May the road of your life lead you back to my kitchen often; I have many love letters to bake for you.

To Emma, my beautiful helper, I treasure our time together, cooking, baking, and of course, taste testing. I love your enthusiasm for helping! To Travis, Kevin and Hunter, who are always willing to lick the spatula, sneak a spoonful of dough, or check the frosting to make sure it's just right. Your smiles light up my day.

To my husband, Gregg, who has encouraged me, laughed with me, and eaten way too many cookies with me! I love you.

Legal Disclaimer

The information contained in this book is not intended to replace professional medical advice, diagnosis, or treatment. If you suspect that you have a food allergy, seek professional medical care. Any use of the information in this book is at the reader's discretion. The author specifically disclaims any and all liability arising directly or indirectly from the application of any information contained in this book.

The reader accepts sole responsibility for the use of the information contained in this book.

Introduction

By Gregg Van Horn

"Gurgle" complained my stomach, as I drove to work, hungry due to the shockingly bare state of our cupboards. I awoke that morning with neither milk for my cereal, nor cereal for my bowl. My 25 year run of milk and cereal for breakfast had come to an abrupt end.

The day before, after a first visit with our son's allergist, my wife and I had purged our kitchen of most of its food, upon learning that our son had life threatening allergies to eggs, peanuts, and tree nuts. On top of that, he had allergies to wheat, soy, and dairy. Neither my wife nor I have food allergies, so it was a shock to learn our 11-month old son had so many of them. We were in unknown territory. We considered nothing safe and feared for our son's safety. "But what's left to eat!?" I wondered.

"Grumble" I quietly protested, during the first month of new foods and adjustments. I like tradition and normalcy, and this didn't fit in either category. We were on shaky ground at first, trying to safely navigate all the allergies (there wasn't a lot of great allergy information out there at the time). Main courses were the first item that had to stabilize. We needed to eat. Beth dove in with a purpose and soon she was cooking safe, healthy meals. And it turns out that a steady diet of nonprocessed meat, potatoes, fruits, and vegetables isn't all that bad…although I quietly wondered when I'd get a homemade cookie again.

* * *

Baking – First Attempts

"Gurkle" said the brownies, as I attempted to cut a piece out of the pan. Beth and I looked at each other and back at the hot gooey sticky mess that no normal person would call edible, let alone brownies. "Ladies first" I offered. We each spooned up a pile of gurkle, and with trepidation, swallowed it down. Our stomachs, realizing they'd been tricked, started protesting immediately with their own gurkles and grumbles. We finished our scoops of "brownies" and shoved the pan away. But once the stomach realized there was a foreign entity in its sanctuary, it began raging a full-on retaliation, planning a risky reverse peristalsis maneuver. We sat very still for the rest of the night, listening with dread to the sounds of war. We survived that long night, but some of those first baked goods are still working their way through my digestive tract today. And I fear the day they finally reach daylight.

We quickly learned that baking without three major ingredients (wheat, eggs, and dairy) is difficult and dangerous, if not impossible. Although, it didn't stop Beth from trying. Cake trickled through our forks, cookies damaged our teeth with their titanium shells and burned our mouths with their steaming liquid centers, and many pans were destroyed when baked goods transformed into caramel massacres.

After several years, Beth's attempts at baked good slowly dwindled, but there was still a desire for our son to have those iconic dessert items that every child should enjoy.

And then came the glorious day, three years after our son was first diagnosed with allergies, that he was pronounced no longer allergic to wheat. We danced and sang and ate bread that didn't taste like dirt. It felt like so many culinary options had just become available. And Beth went to work creating new, delicious, and safe meals in the Wonderful World of Wheat (WWW). Our joy, along with our carbs, skyrocketed.

Several weeks later, after our WWW high had subsided, I leaned over and whispered to Beth "cookies". We both knew this moment would come. But was she ready to face her adversary again after suffering major losses in the first attempts at baking? She was. And with a powerful new weapon in her hands she marched off to wage war, and she has come out victorious beyond our wildest dreams.

* * *

Wheat!

"Great!" exclaimed Aidan, after eating his *first* Birthday cake on his *fourth* Birthday. It was a far cry from his third birthday when we stuck a candle in a halved peach and sang Happy Birthday. The cake wasn't perfect yet, but it was good and tasted like cake. It was a momentous occasion for our family. And we rarely light fruit on fire anymore.

I find it quite amazing that we could go from Gurkle to Great by just adding back in one ingredient. It demonstrates the mad skills of my wife, the baked-good-goddess. But Beth has never been one to be content with good enough. She has worked for the past 6 years perfecting her recipes, tweaking and modifying each one until they were just right. Through her dedication to the art of baking and her love for her family, Beth has created some spectacular desserts: fluffy moist cakes, warm sugar cookies fresh out of the oven that melt in your mouth, and cookie dough so good that we'll keep a batch in the fridge to eat with a spoon (it's egg-free after all!). And I have the honor of being the #1 taste tester, sampling desserts that have become better with each version, until they were perfect and deemed ready for this cookbook. I truly believe that the baked goods in this cookbook are the best allergy-safe desserts you'll ever eat, delicious to even those accustomed to eggs and dairy in their baked goods.

Now, as the husband of the baker, you may think me biased, but these recipes have survived rigorous blind taste tests by a group of professional engineers, architects, surveyors, and secretaries. I have a cubicle directly across from our break room. I often bring in a big plate of baked goods, surreptitiously place it in the break room, and listen as the sharks begin to circle. If the treats are good, they'll hunt down the supplier. If they're bad (a rarity), word spreads quickly, and the cookies get a verbal lashing that would make a construction worker blush.

A colleague of mine, we'll call him Bob, tried the chocolate chip cookies I brought in one morning. After his first one he sent out the siren call (usually a series of muffled moans). Two more people soon arrived and began devouring cookies. And during a break in the feeding frenzy, I heard Bob whisper to the other two, "Let's eat them all!!"

After Bob's fourth cookie and some more blissful moaning, he decided he must find the supplier. By the time I confessed he was on his eighth cookie, and admitted to maybe overdoing it, "My lunch and my waistline are ruined!" he cried as he shook me by the shoulders. I watched him storm off, taking a shortcut through the break room, grabbing his ninth and tenth cookies. Later, after the cookies were gone and his sugar high had subsided, I told him that the cookies were egg and dairy free. He didn't believe me, but sat at his desk slack-jawed pleading for me to bring more in.

* * *

Tested and tried, the recipes in this cookbook have been enjoyed by friends, family, and colleagues alike. But first and foremost, these recipes are Beth's love letters to her children, especially those with allergies. So please enjoy these delicious baked goods, knowing that they are the result of years of work, created out of love, and *safe* for your loved ones with allergies.

Table of Contents

Getting Started

There are a few things to keep in mind as you get started. Let's begin with safety. While our home is egg-free, dairy-free, and peanut/tree nut-free, yours might not be. To avoid any potential cross-contamination with possible allergens:

- READ LABELS! The best way to know if a certain brand of an ingredient is safe, is to READ the LABEL every time you purchase the product. If the ingredient has a "May contain" statement, or "Processed on the same equipment as…" choose something else! It is better to be safe than sorry. If you have any doubt at all, call the manufacturer.
- Wash your equipment and baking gear thoroughly with dish soap and water.
- Scrub your countertops and give yourself a clean, non-contaminated place to work.

These simple steps can make all the difference.

It is also important to remember that oven temperatures vary, so check on your baked goods 2 minutes before the recommended baking time is up. If your oven runs hot, the baked goods will finish sooner than the time given in the recipes; if it runs cold, you will need to extend the baking time.

There are several "must have items" for baking that I strongly recommend investing in if you are just starting on your allergy-safe baking journey. You probably already have most of them in your kitchen!

- Electric stand mixer, with a dough hook, paddle attachment, and whisk attachment
- Non-stick spatulas – I like to have several sizes, and kids' sizes so they can help in the kitchen!
- Cookie scoops, various sizes – I most often use a size 20 (3 Tablespoons), and a size 60 (2 teaspoons)
- Dough cutter
- Wire whisk
- Several mixing bowls – small, medium, large
- Liquid measuring cups
- Dry measuring cups
- Baking sheets
- 9x13 baking dish
- Muffin tins
- Mini-muffin tins
- Microplane for zesting
- Quality ingredients – when available, and when you can afford it, buy organic ingredients. The higher the quality ingredient that you use, the higher the quality dessert or baked good you will produce.

I am so pleased to be able to share my family's favorite baked goods and desserts with you. These recipes are the result of nine years of experimenting in the kitchen, numerous (and epic) failures, and a fierce determination to give my children a sense of "normal" surrounding food.

Baking without dairy or eggs can be a very intimidating task, and I hope that this cookbook makes it simple and rewarding. I have done the hard work of finding the right substitutions, and adjusting the ratios in classic recipes, so all you have to do is enjoy the experience of baking amazing treats for your food allergic family and friends.

Last but not least, the baked goods and desserts you are about to make are each a love letter to my children. With each bite, I hope they feel the love that went into creating a safe and delicious treat for them. When you make these recipes in your own home, they become a love letter to your food allergic loved one, to the child in the class who has a food allergy, to the mom who worries that food might steal her child's life, to each person affected by food allergies. So, share the love, and as always, from "The Allergy Safe Kitchen" I wish you,

"Good Cooking, and Safe Eating!"

Beth Anne Van Horn

Ingredient Notes:

It can be daunting to find safe ingredients if you have never had to look for them before. At the time of my writing this cookbook, the following items are the ones that I feed my own family. Please note, it is vitally important to read the label each and every time you purchase a product. Companies can change their formulas without warning. As I stated earlier, if you have any doubt as to whether or not a product is safe, call the manufacturer.

When the recipe calls for:	We use:
Dairy-free margarine	*Earth Balance* Bars
Dairy-free chocolate morsels	*Enjoy Life* Chocolate Morsels or Chunks, *Wegmans* chocolate morsels
Sunflower Seed Spread	*Sunbutter*
Vegetable Shortening	*Crisco*
Flax Milk	*Good Karma* flax milk

In addition to reading labels, please be aware that cross-contamination is enough to cause a life-threatening reaction for those who have severe food allergies. That means, if you put a knife that spread peanut butter into a jar of jelly, that jar of jelly is now contaminated, and NOT safe for a peanut allergic individual. Any open container of food can become cross-contaminated with the simple transfer of a utensil. If there is ANY doubt about the safety of an already open container, use a brand new one when cooking for your food allergic loved one!

*Every recipe in this cookbook is written to be free of any eggs, dairy, peanuts, or tree nuts. *Check the ingredient lists and your local products to make sure that these recipes are allergy safe for your family and/or friends!*

Cookies

Gingerbread Men

Ingredients:
1 cup vegetable shortening
½ cup dairy-free margarine
1/3 cup granulated sugar
1/3 cup molasses
2 ½ cups unbleached all-purpose flour
1 teaspoon ground ginger
¾ teaspoon ground cinnamon
¼ teaspoon ground allspice
½ teaspoon baking soda
¼ teaspoon salt

Directions:
1. In an electric stand mixer fitted with a paddle attachment, cream together the shortening, margarine, granulated sugar, and molasses.
2. In a separate bowl, whisk together the flour, ginger, cinnamon, allspice, baking soda, and salt.
3. Add the flour mixture to the mixer slowly and beat until fully incorporated.
4. Cover the dough with plastic wrap and refrigerate for at least an hour.
5. Preheat oven to 375 degrees F.
6. Take half the dough out to work with at a time.
7. On a lightly floured surface, roll the dough out to ¼ inch thick. Cut using medium sized cookie cutters.
8. Place cookies on ungreased cookie sheets and bake for 10 minutes.
9. Remove to cooling racks to cool completely.
10. Decorate with icing and sprinkles!

Christmas Cutouts

This is perhaps, the recipe that I become the most emotional about. I have wonderful childhood memories of being in the kitchen with my mother, rolling out dough, getting flour practically everywhere in the kitchen, adding just a little more anise extract than we should, and listening to "Fred Waring and the Pennslyvanians, Christmas Magic." I knew, even before I was married, that THIS was a tradition I would carry on with my own children. The first Christmas after my son was diagnosed with food allergies, I didn't know if I would ever be blessed with the chance to bake Christmas cutouts with my children, to carry on that tradition. For years, I missed that warm feeling and it was really the only "food experience" I think I mourned. The first Christmas after he outgrew the wheat allergy, my mom and dad came over and all of us baked and decorated, together. The last time we made these cookies, my son came into the kitchen while they were baking and said: "It smells like Christmas!" Yes, yes it does. It is now a tradition that my parents come over to decorate these cookies with us each year. It has become a celebration of family, hope, and how far we have come in this food allergy journey. It is with a full heart that I share this recipe with you.

Ingredients:

½ cup dairy-free margarine

1 ½ cup vegetable shortening

2 ¼ cup granulated sugar

4 Tablespoons flax milk

1 Tablespoon pure anise extract

6 Tablespoons vegetable oil, 6 Tablespoons water, 1
     Tablespoon aluminum free baking powder
     (Whisk together in a mug until frothy and add as one
     ingredient. This is your egg substitute.)

6 cups unbleached all-purpose flour
1 ½ Tablespoons aluminum-free baking powder
¾ teaspoon salt

Directions:

1. In an electric stand mixer, fitted with a paddle attachment, cream together the margarine, shortening, sugar, anise, and flax milk.
2. Add egg substitute and mix until fully combined.
3. In a separate bowl, whisk together the flour, baking powder, and salt.
4. Add the dry ingredients to the wet mixture in three batches, mixing completely after each addition.
5. Cover the dough tightly in plastic wrap. Refrigerate for at least 4 hours.
6. Preheat oven to 375 degrees F. Lightly flour your working surface.
7. Remove part of the dough and roll it out to about ¼ inch thick.
8. Cut out using cookie cutters. Lift cookies off the work surface with a large offset spatula and place on ungreased baking sheets. (Cutters that are no more than 5 inches at their longest/widest work best.)
9. Bake 8-10 minutes. Let cool on baking sheets for 1-2 minutes.
10. Remove to cooling racks to cool completely before frosting.
11. Frost using the Decorating Frosting on page 96. Replace the pure vanilla extract in the recipe with pure anise extract. Decorate with your favorite sprinkles!

Big Hit Chocolate Chip Cookies

Who doesn't love chocolate chip cookies warm from the oven? Every mom should have a chocolate chip recipe in her arsenal! This one is mine, and I hope it becomes a dessert staple in your house too. I make it often, and sometimes we just eat the dough! (It's egg-free, no salmonella!)

Ingredients:

½ cup dairy-free margarine (cold)
½ cup vegetable shortening
½ cup granulated sugar
¼ cup light brown sugar
¾ cup dark brown sugar
1 ½ teaspoon pure vanilla extract
3 Tablespoons vegetable oil, 3 Tablespoons water, ½ Tablespoon aluminum - free baking powder (Whisk together in a mug until frothy and add as one ingredient. This is your egg substitute.)
2 ¾ cups of unbleached flour
1 teaspoon baking powder
½ teaspoon salt
1 ½ cups of dairy-free chocolate morsels

Directions:
1. Preheat oven to 380 degrees F
2. Cream together cold margarine and shortening.
3. Add sugar, brown sugars, vanilla extract, and continue creaming until well incorporated.
4. Add egg substitute and blend well.

5. In a separate bowl, whisk together flour, baking powder, and salt.
6. Slowly add dry mixture to wet ingredients and blend until fully incorporated.
7. Stir in the chocolate morsels with a spatula.
8. Eat the batter – it's egg-free, no salmonella!!
9. Using a 2 teaspoon cookie scoop (size 60), scoop dough directly onto a cookie sheet about two to three inches apart.
10. Bake for 10-12 minutes.
11. Let cookies cool on the cookie sheet for a few minutes and then remove them to cooking racks to cool completely.

Variations:

- Spread all cookie dough into a greased 9x13 pan. Bake at 380 degrees F for 20 – 25 minutes. Cut into cookie bars for serving!
- Scoop onto a wax lined paper-lined cookie sheet. Freeze for 30 minutes and then package in a zip-top bag and return to freezer. When you want a snack, take cookies out and place on cookie sheet while the oven is pre-heating. Bake as usual!
- Divide dough in half. Form each half into a log and roll in parchment paper. Wrap in saran wrap, then foil, and then freeze! Take out frozen dough rolls and slice cookies about ½ thick. Bake as usual.

Snow Kissed Cookies

*Bring a little winter into your kitchen with these gorgeous cookies.
They turn out a deep chocolate color with a crackled white sugar
coating, and they are just as wonderful to eat as they are to look at!
Add them to your holiday table, or make them any time.*

Ingredients:
1 ¼ cups light brown sugar
1 cup vegetable shortening
1 teaspoon pure vanilla extract
3 Tablespoons vegetable oil, 3 Tablespoons water, ½
Tablespoon aluminum free baking powder (Whisk together
in a mug until frothy and add as one ingredient. This is your egg
substitute.)
2 cups unbleached all-purpose flour
3 Tablespoons dark cocoa powder
3 Tablespoons unsweetened cocoa powder
½ teaspoon kosher salt
¼ teaspoon baking soda
¾ cup dairy-free chocolate mini-morsels
1/3 cup granulated sugar
½ cup confectioners' sugar

Directions:
1. In a stand mixer, cream together brown sugar, shortening, and vanilla extract.
2. Add the egg substitute and beat until mixture is fluffy and light.
3. In a separate bowl, whisk flour, cocoa powders, salt, and baking soda until uniform in color.

4. Add this dry mixture slowly to the wet mixture and beat on medium until fully incorporated.
5. Cover dough tightly with plastic wrap, and chill for 2 hours.
6. Preheat oven to 375 degrees F. Measure granulated sugar into a bowl, and the confectioners' sugar into a separate bowl.
7. Using a 2 teaspoon cookie scoop (size 60), scoop dough and roll into balls.
8. Roll each ball first in the granulated sugar, and then in the confectioners' sugar to completely coat.
9. Space about 2 inches apart and bake for 8-10 minutes on an ungreased baking sheet.
10. Let the cookies cool for 3 minutes on the baking sheet, and then remove to a cooling rack.

Hint: Kids LOVE to roll these cookies in the sugar; get them into the kitchen for some quality time with you!

Chocolate Pretzel Cookies

All of the salty-sweet goodness of a chocolate-covered pretzel, in a cookie! I love the contrast of chocolate and salt, and these cookies satisfy that desire for me every time. So simple, so special, a perfect take-a-long to any party or gathering!

Ingredients:
Cookie dough:
¾ cup vegetable shortening
¼ cup dairy-free margarine
¾ cup light brown sugar
½ cup dark brown sugar
3 Tablespoons vegetable oil, 3 Tablespoons water, ½
   Tablespoon aluminum-free baking powder (Whisk
   together in a mug until frothy and add as one ingredient.
   This is your egg substitute.)
1 teaspoon pure vanilla extract
2 cups unbleached all-purpose flour
½ teaspoon baking soda
¼ teaspoon kosher salt
Topping:
10 ounce bag dairy-free chocolate morsels
½ Tablespoon vegetable shortening
crushed pretzels

Directions:
1. Preheat the oven to 350 degree F.
2. In an electric stand mixer, fitted with the paddle attachment, cream together the shortening, margarine, and sugars.

3. Add egg substitute and vanilla extract and beat until fluffy.
4. In a separate bowl, whisk together flour, salt, and baking soda.
5. Add dry ingredients to the wet mixture and beat until fully incorporated
6. Using a 2 teaspoon (size 60) cookie scoop, scoop dough and place on baking sheets.
7. Bake for 12 minutes. Let cool for several minutes on the baking sheets and then remove to cooling racks to cool completely.
8. Make the topping. Melt morsels and shortening in a microwave safe bowl, stirring at 30 second intervals.
9. Dip the tops of the cookies into the melted chocolate.
10. While chocolate is still wet on top of the cookies, sprinkle with crushed pretzels. Gently press pretzel pieces into the chocolate to set firmly in place.
11. Let chocolate set for about 40 minutes, and enjoy!

Little Puckers

Sometimes dessert needs a little pucker to it! Every once in a while, I get a hankering for a lighter, more refreshing, dessert. These cookies are sweet and lemony and delicious!

Ingredients:
Dough:
2 cups unbleached all-purpose flour
¼ teaspoon baking soda
¼ teaspoon salt
12 Tablespoons dairy-free margarine
1 ¼ cups granulated sugar
1 Tablespoon lemon zest
3 Tablespoons vegetable oil, 3 Tablespoons water, ½
     Tablespoon aluminum free baking powder (Whisk
     together in a mug until frothy and add as one ingredient.
     This is your egg substitute.)
¾ teaspoon lemon extract
¾ teaspoon orange extract
Glaze:
1 cup confectioners' sugar
3 Tablespoons fresh lemon juice
½ Tablespoon lemon zest

Directions:
Dough:
1. Combine flour, baking soda, and salt in a bowl and whisk together.
2. In a mixer, cream together the margarine, granulated sugar, and citrus zest.
3. Add in the egg substitute and incorporated fully.

4. Add in the lemon and orange extracts and blend completely.
5. Slowly add the flour mixture and beat until it yields soft dough.
6. Prepare two baking sheets by lining with parchment paper.
7. Using a 2 teaspoon cookie scoop (size 60), scoop dough onto the prepared baking sheets about two inches apart.
8. Place baking sheets in the freezer for 30 minutes.
9. Preheat the oven to 375 degrees F.
10. Bake cookies, one baking sheet at a time, for 15 minutes. (Do NOT thaw before placing baking sheet in oven!)
11. Let cool briefly on the baking sheet and then remove to a cooling rack to cool completely.

Glaze:
1. Whisk the confectioners' sugar, 2 Tablespoons of the lemon juice, and ½ Tablespoon lemon zest together in a bowl. Thin the glaze to desired consistency using the remaining Tablespoon of lemon juice.
2. Spread the glaze onto the cookies and let them set on a cooling rack for about an hour.

Variations:

- Use orange, lime, or grapefruit instead of lemons.
- Use Meyer lemons when they are in season!

Giant Double Chocolate Cookies

Decadent, rich, perfect for a special occasion, these cookies are divine!

Ingredients:
2 ½ cups unbleached flour
¾ cup unsweetened cocoa powder
½ cup dark cocoa powder
2 Tablespoons organic cornstarch
½ teaspoon Kosher salt
¾ teaspoon baking powder (aluminum free)
½ teaspoon baking soda
½ cup dairy free margarine
½ cup butter flavored shortening
1 teaspoon pure vanilla extract
¾ cup light brown sugar
¾ cup dark brown sugar
½ cup granulated sugar
6 Tablespoons vegetable oil, 6 Tablespoons water, 1 Tablespoon
  Aluminum-free baking powder (Whisk together in a mug
  until frothy and add as one ingredient. This is your egg
  substitute.)
1 ½ cups dairy free chocolate morsels

Directions:
1. Whisk together flour, cornstarch, salt, cocoa powders, baking powder, and baking soda until this dry mix is uniform in color.
2. Using a mixer, cream the margarine, shortening, vanilla extract, brown sugars, and granulated sugar. Beat until the largest lumps are pea sized.

3. Add in the egg substitute and beat until incorporated.
4. Add the dry mix slowly and beat until fully combined.
5. Stir in the chocolate morsels with a spatula.
6. Cover by placing plastic wrap directly on the surface of the dough to prevent drying and refrigerate for at least 2 hours. (You can let this dough chill overnight.)
7. Preheat oven to 375 degrees F.
8. Line two cookie sheets with parchment paper.
9. Using a 3 Tablespoon scoop (size 20): Scoop to ensure even measurement, and GENTLY roll the dough into large balls with your hands. Do not overwork the dough or compact it too much. (Makes 12 LARGE cookies)
10. Bake for 14 minutes, rotate cookie sheets halfway through baking.
11. Turn off the oven off and let the cookies rest inside for 5 more minutes.
12. Remove the cookies and let them set on the cookie sheets for 10 more minutes.
13. Transfer cookies to a cooling rack and cool completely.

Variations:

- Make "ice cream" sandwiches with these giant cookies. Use your family's favorite soy or coconut ice cream. Soften it slightly to spread on the bottom of one cookie, place a second cookie on top to make a sandwich. Chill in the freezer until "ice cream" sets.
- Alternate egg substitute: Combine 2 Tablespoons white chia seeds with 6 Tablespoons water and let soak for 15 minutes, stirring occasionally. This will result in a cookie that hardly flattens in the oven. They turn out chewy and tall!

Hint: 1 Tablespoon chia seeds, soaked (and mixed) in 3 Tablespoons water is a great substitute for 1 egg!

Giant Chocolate Chip Cookies

Ingredients:

3 3/4 cups unbleached flour

2 Tablespoons organic cornstarch

1 teaspoon Kosher salt

¾ teaspoon baking powder (aluminum free)

½ teaspoon baking soda

½ cup dairy free margarine

½ cup butter flavored shortening

1 teaspoon pure vanilla extract

¾ cup light brown sugar

¾ cup dark brown sugar

½ cup granulated sugar

6 Tablespoons vegetable oil, 6 Tablespoons water, 1 Tablespoon
    Aluminum - free baking powder (Whisk together in a
    mug until frothy and add as one ingredient. This is your egg
    substitute.)

1 ½ cups dairy free chocolate morsels

Directions:

1. Whisk together flour, cornstarch, salt, baking powder,
   and baking soda.
2. Using a mixer, cream the margarine, shortening, vanilla
   extract, brown sugars, and granulated sugar. Beat until
   the largest lumps are pea sized.
3. Add in the egg substitute and beat until incorporated.
4. Add the dry mix slowly and beat until fully combined.
5. Stir in the chocolate morsels with a spatula.

6. Cover by placing plastic wrap directly on the surface of the dough to prevent drying and refrigerate for at least 2 hours. (You can let this dough chill overnight.)
7. Preheat oven to 375 degrees F.
8. Line two cookie sheets with parchment paper.
9. Using a 3 Tablespoon scoop (size 20): Scoop to ensure even measurement, and GENTLY roll the dough into large balls with your hands. Do not overwork the dough or compact it too much. (Makes 12 LARGE cookies)
10. Bake until the cookies are just barely golden at the edges, about 18-20 minutes, rotate cookie sheets halfway through baking.
11. Turn off the oven off and let the cookies rest inside for 5 more minutes.
12. Remove the cookies and let them set on the cookie sheets for 10 more minutes.
13. Transfer cookies to a cooling rack and cool completely.

Variations:

- Make "ice cream" sandwiches with these giant cookies. Use your family's favorite soy or coconut ice cream. Soften it slightly to spread on the bottom of one cookie, place a second cookie on top to make a sandwich. Chill in the freezer until "ice cream" sets.
- Alternate egg substitute: Combine 2 Tablespoons white chia seeds with 6 Tablespoons water and let soak for 15 minutes, stirring occasionally. This will result in a cookie that hardly flattens in the oven. They turn out chewy and tall!

Over the Top Oatmeal Cookies

I created these cookies when a ridiculously strong post-pregnancy craving set in. I made four or five batches of cookies in 3 days, trying to get it just right; my kids thought I was the best mom ever! The cinnamon glaze really puts the cookies "over the top"!

Ingredients:
Cookies:
½ cup dairy-free margarine
½ cup shortening
1 1/3 cups light brown sugar
6 Tablespoons of water mixed with 2 Tablespoons white
      Chia seeds (Let this mixture sit for about 10 minutes to allow
      the gel to form. This is your egg substitute.)
1 teaspoon pure vanilla extract
1 ½ cups unbleached all-purpose flour
1 teaspoon baking soda
1 teaspoon ground cinnamon
¾ teaspoon salt
3 cups rolled oats
2 cups raisins
1 cup dairy-free chocolate morsels
Glaze:
2 cups confectioners' sugar
2 Tablespoons ground cinnamon
1/3 cup water or flax/soy milk

Directions:
1. In an electric mixer fitted with the paddle attachment, cream together the margarine, shortening, light brown sugar, chia seed mixture, and vanilla.

38

2. Whisk the flour, salt, baking soda, and cinnamon together in a separate bowl.
3. With the mixer on low-medium speed, combine the flour mixture with the wet ingredients until fully incorporated.
4. Add the oats and mix well.
5. Add the raisins and chocolate morsels and stir them in by hand.
6. Cover the bowl of dough with plastic wrap and chill in the fridge for ½ hour.
7. Preheat the oven to 350 degrees F and prepare two baking sheets by lining them with parchment paper.
8. Using a 2 teaspoon (size 60) cookie scoop, scoop and drop the cookies onto a baking sheet. Flatten the tops slightly with the back of the scoop.
9. Bake for 10-12 minutes. Cool on the baking sheets for 4 minutes and then remove to cooling racks to cool completely.
10. Make the glaze. Whisk together the confectioners' sugar, cinnamon and water.
11. Using a spoon or small spatula, drizzle the glaze over the tops of the cookies while they are on the cooling racks. *Placing foil or waxed paper under the cooling racks will catch any drips and make cleanup a lot easier!

Spritz Cookies

A cookie press is needed to make these fun and simple cookies. Make several batches and try different shapes, natural food colorings, and extract flavors to make a gorgeous cookie platter without enormous effort!

Ingredients:
1 ½ cups butter flavored vegetable shortening
1 cup granulated sugar
3 Tablespoons water, 3 Tablespoons oil, ½ Tablespoon
aluminum-free baking powder (Whisk together in a mug until frothy and add to the cookie dough as one ingredient. This is your egg substitute.)
3 Tablespoons soy milk
1 teaspoon pure vanilla extract
½ teaspoon artificial almond extract
3 ½ cups unbleached all-purpose flour
1 teaspoon baking powder

Directions:
1. Preheat oven to 375 degrees F.
2. In a stand mixer fitted with a whisk attachment, cream together the shortening and sugar.
3. Add the egg substitute, vanilla extract, and soy milk. Mix until fully incorporated.
4. In a separate bowl, whisk together the flour and baking powder.
5. Slowly add flour mixture to wet ingredients, scraping the sides of the mixing bowl as needed. Mix until a smooth dough is formed.

6. Fill your cookie press, and press cookies onto ungreased baking sheets according to manufacturer's directions. *
7. Bake for 10 – 12 minutes, or until just barely light brown at the edges.
8. Remove to cooling racks to cool completely.

Some cookie presses require just one click for one cookie, others require two clicks for one cookie. I find that the two click method has worked better for us regardless of brand.

Mega-Mash-Up Cookies

Chewy and crunchy, these cookies have it all! My kids love to "spatter" the chocolate topping onto the cookies!

Ingredients:

Cookie dough:

2 cups of unbleached all-purpose flour

1 teaspoon aluminum-free baking powder

½ teaspoon baking soda

½ cup butter flavored vegetable shortening

½ cup dairy-free margarine

1 cup granulated sugar

½ cup light brown sugar

½ cup dark brown sugar

6 Tablespoons vegetable oil, 6 Tablespoons water, 1 Tablespoon aluminum free baking powder (Whisk together in a mug until frothy and add as one ingredient. This is your egg substitute.)

1 Tablespoon pure vanilla extract

2 cups oats

2 ¼ cups crispy rice cereal

1 ½ cups dairy-free chocolate chunks

¾ cup mini marshmallows

¾ cup raisins or dried cranberries

Topping:

1 ½ cups dairy-free chocolate morsels

½ Tablespoon vegetable shortening

1/8 teaspoon ancho chili powder

1/8 teaspoon ground cinnamon

Directions:

1. Preheat the oven to 350 degree F.

42

2. Prepare baking sheets by lining with parchment paper or non-stick silicone baking mats.
3. In an electric stand mixer, fitted with the paddle attachment, cream together the shortening, margarine, and sugars.
4. Add egg substitute and vanilla extract and beat until just fluffy.
5. In a separate bowl, whisk together flour, baking powder, and baking soda.
6. Add dry ingredients to the wet mixture in two batches, mixing completely after each addition.
7. Transfer dough into a larger bowl and stir in the oats, crispy rice cereal, chocolate chunks, mini marshmallows, and raisins. Make sure the add-ins are evenly mixed throughout the dough.
8. Using a 3 Tablespoon cookie scoop, scoop dough and pack it into the scoop before releasing onto the baking sheets. Leave about 2-3 inches in between cookies, they spread a fair amount.
9. Bake for 15 minutes. Remove from oven and slide the parchment or baking mat onto a cooling rack. Let cookies cool for at least 10 minutes before removing from parchment.
10. Make the topping. Combine all ingredients in a microwave safe bowl and melt, stirring at 30 second intervals.
11. Using a fork or spoon, drizzle the cookies with "spattered" chocolate by wiggling the spoon back and forth quickly over the cookies.
12. Let chocolate set for about 40 minutes, and enjoy!

Big Hit Cookie Cake

This is my husband's creation. He requested it for his birthday last year, and we all agreed: he's pretty brilliant!

Ingredients:
Double batch of *Big Hit Chocolate Chip Cookie* dough, *page 26*
Single batch of *Chocolate Non-buttercream Frosting, page 97*
Single batch of *"Sunbutter" Frosting, page 98*

Directions:
1. Press cookie dough into two round disposable pizza pans. (Use the kind without vent holes in the bottom!)
2. Bake at 350 degrees F for 30 minutes.
3. After allowing them to cool completely, carefully turn one "cookie" out onto a tray. Spread a thick layer of "Sunbutter" Frosting onto the cookie.
4. Carefully place the second "cookie" on top of the frosting.
5. Using a piping bag and the decorating tip of your choice, pipe a border along the top of the second cookie with the Chocolate "Non-buttercream" Frosting.
6. Use up the frostings by decorating the remainder of the cookie cake however you wish!

We found that letting the cake sit for about an hour before serving gave the frosting a chance to soften the cookie a little.

Muffins, Breads, and Pastries

Basic Muffins

Use this recipe as a base for a multitude of muffins! Add in spices you love, fruits, or flavored extracts to have a different muffin every morning of the week!

Ingredients:
1 ¾ cups unbleached all-purpose flour
¾ teaspoon salt
¼ cup granulated sugar
2 teaspoons baking powder
6 Tablespoons vegetable oil, 6 Tablespoons water, 1 Tablespoon Aluminum-free baking powder (Whisk together in a mug until frothy and add as one ingredient. This is your egg substitute.)
¾ cup Flax or Soy milk
3 Tablespoons melted margarine

Directions:
1. Preheat oven to 400 degrees F.
2. Prepare 2 muffin tins by greasing well with margarine or shortening.
3. In a mixing bowl, whisk together flour, salt, sugar, and baking powder.
4. In a separate bowl, combine egg substitute, Flax milk, and melted margarine.
5. Gently stir the wet mixture into the dry. Do not over mix! There will be some lumps and that is okay!
6. Using a 3 Tablespoon (size 20) scoop, divide the batter between the muffin tins.
7. Bake for 20 -25 minutes.

Blueberry Muffins

These muffins are perfect for breakfast or a brunch buffet!

Ingredients:

3 1/2 cups unbleached all-purpose flour

1 ½ teaspoons salt

2/3 cup granulated sugar

4 teaspoons baking powder

6 Tablespoons vegetable oil, 6 Tablespoons water, 1 Tablespoon
Aluminum-free baking powder (Whisk together in a mug
until frothy and add as one ingredient. This is your egg
substitute.)

1 ½ cups Flax or Soy milk

½ cup melted dairy-free margarine

2 teaspoons fresh lemon zest

1 teaspoon pure vanilla extract

2 cups fresh blueberries, dredged in flour

Directions:

1. Preheat oven to 400 degrees F.
2. Prepare 2 muffin tins by greasing well with margarine or
   shortening.
3. In a mixing bowl, whisk together flour, salt, sugar, and
   baking powder.
4. In a separate bowl, combine egg substitute, Flax milk, melted
   margarine, vanilla, and lemon zest.
5. Gently stir the wet mixture into the dry. Do not over mix!
   Fold the blueberries into the batter before the batter is totally
   moist. There will be some lumps and that is okay!

6. Using a 3 Tablespoon (size 20) scoop, divide the batter between the muffin tins.
7. Bake for 20 -25 minutes.
8. Let cool for 2-3 minutes in the tins, and then remove to a cooling rack to cool completely.

Variations:

- Mix ½ cup sugar and 1 Tablespoon cinnamon in a small bowl. Sprinkle over the muffins before baking. This is our favorite way to make them!

Pumpkin Muffins

Autumn wouldn't be complete without some pumpkin goodies. Add these muffins to your Thanksgiving spread, or enjoy them any time you want to embrace the flavors of Fall.

Ingredients:
1 ¾ cups unbleached all-purpose flour
¾ teaspoon salt
½ cup granulated sugar
2 teaspoons baking powder
2 teaspoons pumpkin pie spice (page 134)
6 Tablespoons vegetable oil, 6 Tablespoons water, 1 Tablespoon
   Aluminum-free baking powder (Whisk together in a mug
   until frothy and add as one ingredient. This is your egg
   substitute.)
¾ cup Flax or Soy milk
3 Tablespoons melted margarine
1 cup canned or fresh (mashed) pumpkin
2 teaspoons orange zest

Directions:
1. Preheat oven to 400 degrees F.
2. Prepare 2 muffin tins by greasing well with margarine or shortening.
3. In a mixing bowl, whisk together flour, salt, sugar, baking powder, and pumpkin pie spice.
4. In a separate bowl, combine egg substitute, Flax milk, melted margarine, pumpkin, and orange zest.

5. Gently stir the wet mixture into the dry. Do not over mix! There will be some lumps and that is okay!
6. Using a 3 Tablespoon (size 20) scoop, divide the batter between the muffin tins.
7. Bake for 20 -25 minutes.
8. Let muffins cool for 2-3 minutes in the tins and then remove to a cooling rack to cool completely.

Variations:
- Use mashed sweet potatoes in place of pumpkin.
- Use mashed butternut squash in place of pumpkin.

Snickerdoodle Mini Muffins

*My kids are fans of anything with cinnamon, so these mini-muffins
make a great mid-morning snack in our home. They love to sprinkle
the topping on before I pop the muffins in the oven. Since the baking
time is only 10 minutes, this is an easy treat for me to whip together
on the spur of the moment*
.

Ingredients:

Muffins:

1 ¾ cups unbleached all-purpose flour

¾ teaspoon salt

¼ cup granulated sugar

2 teaspoons baking powder

¾ teaspoon freshly grated nutmeg

¾ teaspoon baking soda

6 Tablespoons vegetable oil, 6 Tablespoons water, 1 Tablespoon
  Aluminum-free baking powder (Whisk together in a mug
  until frothy and add as one ingredient. This is your egg
  substitute.)

¾ cup Flax or Soy milk

1 teaspoon pure vanilla extract

3 Tablespoons melted margarine

Topping:

½ cup sugar

1 Tablespoon cinnamon

Directions:

1. Preheat oven to 400 degrees F.
2. In a mixing bowl, whisk together flour, salt, sugar, baking powder, nutmeg, and baking soda.
3. In a separate bowl, combine egg substitute, Flax milk, vanilla extract, and melted margarine.
4. Gently stir the wet mixture into the dry. Do not over mix! There will be some lumps and that is okay!
5. Using a 2 teaspoon scoop (size 60) scoop, divide the batter between 2 mini-muffin tins.
6. Combine sugar and cinnamon for the topping. Sprinkle it liberally over the batter in the tins.
7. Bake for 10 minutes.
8. Cool in the tins for 2-3 minutes and then remove to a cooling rack to cool completely.

Mmm, mmm, Muffins

Ingredients:
Muffins:
4 cups of flour
½ cup sugar
2 Tablespoons baking powder
¼ cup dairy-free margarine
½ cup vegetable shortening
2 cups orange marmalade
1 cup orange juice
2 teaspoons pure vanilla extract
¼ teaspoon salt
Powdered egg replacer, use the equivalent of 3 eggs (follow
      manufacturer's directions)
Topping:
½ cup sugar
¼ cup light brown sugar
1 teaspoon cinnamon
¼ teaspoon nutmeg
¼ teaspoon salt
3 Tablespoons dairy-free margarine

Directions:
1. Preheat oven to 375 degrees F.
2. In a bowl, mix together the flour, sugar, and baking powder.
3. Cut in the shortening and dairy-free margarine with a pastry cutter.
4. In a separate bowl, mix together the marmalade, orange juice, and vanilla. Then add to dry mixture and mix until just barely incorporated.

5. Add the egg replacer and mix in gently.
6. Using a large scoop, fill muffin pans evenly.
7. Make the crumble by mixing all the topping ingredients into a bowl.
8. Top each muffin with crumble.
9. Bake for 20 minutes.
10. Cool muffin tins on a cooling rack, and remove muffins from pan as soon as you can handle them.

<u>Hint:</u> Make these muffins the night before, after the kids go to bed, and have a homemade breakfast for your family on any weekday!

Banana Muffins

Ingredients:
6 mashed bananas
1 cup granulated sugar
3/4 cup canola oil
1 ½ teaspoon pure vanilla extract
3 cups unbleached all-purpose flour
¾ cup whole wheat flour
1 ½ teaspoon baking soda
2 Tablespoons baking powder
1 Tablespoon ground cinnamon
Pinch of kosher salt

Directions:
1. Preheat the oven to 325 degrees F.
2. Prepare muffin tin by lining with cupcake liners, or grease and flour. (Makes 32 muffins)
3. In a mixing bowl, combine mashed bananas, sugar, and canola oil.
4. Add the remaining ingredients and mix until just incorporated. Do not over mix, the muffins will get tough.
5. Scoop batter into the muffin tins, filling about 2/3 of the way up.
6. Bake for 25-30 minutes.
7. Remove muffins to a cooling rack to cool.
8. Serve warm with Vanilla Honey Spread, (page 114)

Chocolate Chip Muffins

Make the recipe for Blueberry Muffins (page 48), eliminating the lemon zest, and replacing the 2 cups of blueberries with 1 ½ cups of dairy-free chocolate morsels.

Variations:
- For an extra treat, dip the tops of the chocolate chip muffins in a sugar glaze. To make the sugar glaze, mix 2 cups of confectioners' sugar with 3 Tablespoons of water or Flax/Soy milk, and 1 teaspoon pure vanilla extract.
- To make Orange Chocolate Chip muffins, add the zest of one orange (use a microplane), to the chocolate chip muffin batter. For a special occasion, make an Orange Glaze and drizzle lightly over the tops of the muffins. To make the glaze: whisk together 1 ¼ cups confectioners' sugar, 2 Tablespoons freshly squeezed orange juice.

Basic Pizza Dough

One of the great things about this dough, is that if you double or triple this recipe and freeze the dough balls, you can have enough fresh, safe pizza dough to have one pizza night a week for the entire month! One afternoon of preparation can set you up for success for a month! Use the dough to make calzones, and other dough based treats. Food allergy families know just how expensive organic and allergy friendly convenience foods can be. This dough can offer convenience in the kitchen without breaking the budget!

When you want to have a pizza night, simply take the dough ball out of the freezer in the morning. Place the frozen dough in a large bowl. Coat the ball of dough lightly with a fresh layer of extra-virgin olive oil. Cover the bowl with a damp cloth or kitchen towel and leave it alone on a counter for 4 to 8 hours. At dinner-time, you'll be all set to go! You can top it and bake it in as much time as it takes to order take-out!

Ingredients:
1 1/3 cup warm water
1 Tablespoon granulated sugar
1 packet of active dry yeast
3 Tablespoons extra-virgin olive oil
3 ¾ cups unbleached all-purpose flour
1 ½ teaspoon kosher salt

Directions:
1. Dissolve the sugar in the warm water.
2. Sprinkle 1 packet of dry active yeast on top of the water.
3. Wait about 10 minutes, until the yeast is foamy and then stir in the extra-virgin olive oil.
4. Combine flour and salt in a large bowl.
5. Make a well in the middle and add the wet mixture.

6. Stir to combine and then turn the dough out onto a floured surface.
7. Knead for about 5 minutes, or until the ball is smooth and elastic.
8. Form into 2 balls, coat each in olive oil, put in bowls and cover the bowls tightly with plastic wrap.
9. Leave the 2 bowls at room temperature for about 1 1/2 hours until the dough has doubled in size
   *At this point, you can roll out, top, and bake the dough OR you can wrap it in plastic wrap and freeze it for up to a month.

For a regular sized pizza bake at 500 degrees F for 15-20 minutes - depending on topping load and desired crispiness! (When we make 'mini-pizzas' we start checking them at 10 minutes.)

Simple White Bread

This bread is simply wonderful. It was one of the first bread recipes I learned to make after Aidan outgrew his wheat allergy. The very first time I made it, Gregg and I sat in the kitchen eating it, warm from the oven, and moaning! We were so excited to have something other than "rice bread". This was before the big gluten-free product boom, so our options had been so few for so long...this bread was like our reawakening to baked goods that taste good! We like to eat it warm with some dairy-free margarine; it really doesn't need anything else!

Ingredients:
2 cups warm water
2/3 cup granulated sugar
1 ½ Tablespoons active dry yeast
1 ½ teaspoons salt
¼ cup canola oil
6 cups unbleached all-purpose flour

Directions:
1. In a large mixing bowl, gently stir together the warm water and sugar until the sugar is completely dissolved.
2. Sprinkle the yeast over the top of the water and stir briefly. Let the mixture sit at room temperature until the yeast is foamy.
3. Add oil and salt to the yeast mixture and then begin adding in the flour a bit at a time.
4. Once all the flour has been added, turn out the dough onto a lightly floured surface and knead for about 5 minutes, or until the dough ball is smooth and elastic.
5. Grease a large bowl with canola oil and place the dough ball in it, turning to coat.

6. Cover the bowl with a damp tea towel and let sit at room temperature for about an hour, or until doubled in size.
7. Grease two loaf pans with canola oil.
8. Turn the dough out and punch down. Knead briefly and divide the dough in half.
9. Shape each half into a loaf, making sure the tops are smooth, and place one in each loaf pan.
10. Let the dough rise for 30 minutes, or until it has risen 1 inch above the rim of the pans.
11. Bake for 30 minutes at 350 degrees F.
12. Remove loaves from pans and cool on cooling racks.

English Muffin Bread

I have always loved an English muffin for breakfast, but the version available in the store has dairy in it. This amazing toasting bread bears a very similar taste, and it is safe for ALL members of our household! After baking this bread, it is important to allow it to cool completely so the texture is right. Bake some today, toast some tomorrow morning!

Ingredients:
6 ¾ teaspoons active dry yeast
3 Tablespoons granulated sugar
2 Tablespoons kosher salt
5 ½ cups warm water (105-115 degrees F)
11 cups unbleached all-purpose flour
Vegetable shortening for greasing loaf pans

Directions:
1. In a large mixing bowl, add the sugar to the warm water, stirring until dissolved.
2. Add the yeast to the water and stir briefly.
3. Add salt and flour and mix until fully incorporated. You may have to mix in the final bit of flour with your hands. The dough will be wet and sticky.
4. Let the dough rise, uncovered, until doubled in size.
5. Prepare four loaf pans by greasing well with vegetable shortening.
6. Punch dough down lightly and divide into four equal portions. Place into the four loaf pans.
7. All dough to rise, uncovered, until it reaches the top of the pans.

8. Bake at 350 degrees F for 45 minutes.
9. Remove loaves from pans and allow them to cool COMPLETELY on a cooling rack before slicing.
10. Slice bread and toast it!

Variations:

- After toasting, slather with a layer of dairy-free margarine and a top layer of strawberry preserves.
- I also like to make warm sandwiches with this bread in my cast iron skillet with a Panini press. Before pressing the sandwich, grease the skillet and the press with reserved bacon fat for an out of this world lunch!

Zucchini Bread

Every year we grow zucchini in our garden, and every year we have LOTS of zucchini. I grate it and drain it, and then I freeze it in 2 cup containers so I can make this bread anytime during the year! The kids love it and they request it often. Buy some organic zucchini seeds, start a garden, grow WAY too many zucchini, and set yourself up to be able to bake this bread all year long!

Ingredients:
3 cups unbleached all-purpose flour
¾ teaspoon aluminum-free baking powder
1 teaspoon kosher salt
1 Tablespoon ground cinnamon
1 teaspoon baking soda
2 cups grated zucchini
3 Tablespoons vegetable oil, 3 Tablespoons water, ½

> Tablespoon aluminum-free baking powder (Whisk together in a mug until frothy and add as one ingredient. This is your egg substitute.)

1 cup canola oil
1 Tablespoon pure vanilla extract
2 cups sugar
(reserved juice from draining the zucchini) *optional*

Directions:
1. Preheat the oven to 350 degrees F.
2. In a mixing bowl, whisk together the flour, baking powder, salt, cinnamon, and baking soda until uniformly combined.

3. Add the remaining ingredients and mix until just incorporated. If the batter seems very dry, use some of the reserved zucchini juice to help incorporate the dry ingredients.
4. Divide batter into three ungreased loaf pans.
5. Bake for 55-60 minutes.

Sweet Dough

This sweet dough is awesome! I use it for so many different treats, and I'm finding more uses for it all the time! People will be amazed at what you can create with this dairy-free, egg-free dough.

Ingredients:
½ cup Flax/Soy milk
2 ¼ teaspoons active dry yeast
¼ cup melted dairy-free margarine
3 Tablespoons vegetable oil, 3 Tablespoons water, ½
    Tablespoon aluminum-free baking powder (Whisk
    together in a mug until frothy and add as one ingredient.
    This is your egg substitute.)
1 ½ teaspoons pure vanilla extract
2 ¾ cups unbleached, all-purpose flour
¼ cup granulated sugar
¾ teaspoon salt

Directions:
1. Gently heat flax/soy milk with ½ cup water until it reaches approximately 110 degrees F.
2. Remove from the heat and sprinkle the yeast and a pinch of sugar over the top. Let this sit until the yeast blooms and becomes foamy. (It should only take about 5 minutes.)
3. While you are waiting for the yeast to bloom, whisk together the flour, sugar, and salt in a large mixing bowl.
4. Melt the margarine in a separate small bowl.
5. Once the yeast mixture is foamy, add the melted margarine, egg substitute, and vanilla to it. Whisk until combined.

6. Stir the wet mixture into the dry mixture. The dough will be thick and a little sticky. Turn it out onto a floured surface and knead for about 5 minutes, until the dough is soft and elastic.
7. Shape the dough into a ball and place into a large bowl that has been greased with dairy-free margarine. Turn the dough to coat.
8. Cover with a damp tea towel and let it rise at room temperature for about an hour, (or longer if need be), until the dough has doubled in size.
9. Turn the dough out of the bowl and knead briefly. Return to the bowl and cover with plastic wrap directly on the surface of the dough ball. Then cover the bowl tightly and refrigerate for 4 hours. You may refrigerate this dough overnight.

Use this dough for the following recipes in this cookbook:
  Cinnamon Swirl Buns
  Mocha Swirl Buns
  Blueberry Lemon Twists
  Monkey Bread
  Twisted Chocolate Loaf

Cinnamon Swirl Buns

*Mmmmm….cinnamon buns. The welcoming smell, the feel of sweet
orange icing oozing over fingertips, the decadent warmth of a
cinnamon bun on a Sunday morning before the kids get up... Ok, stop
drooling, start baking!*

Ingredients:
Buns:
1 batch Sweet Dough (page 66)
12 Tablespoons dairy-free margarine, softened slightly
1/3 cup granulated sugar
2 Tablespoons cinnamon
Icing:
1 ¼ cups confectioners' sugar
3 Tablespoons freshly squeezed orange juice
Zest of one orange

Directions:
1. Grease a 9x13 inch baking dish with dairy-free margarine or shortening.
2. Prepare the filling by whisking together the granulated sugar and cinnamon in a bowl.
3. Roll out the dough into a 10x18 inch rectangle on a lightly floured surface.
4. Using a spatula or an offset spatula spread the dairy-free margarine over the dough. Leave a 1 inch border along one of the long sides.
5. Sprinkle the margarine evenly with the cinnamon sugar.

6. Using your finger, brush the clean border edge with water.
7. Tightly roll the dough toward the clean border edge, and then pinch the seam to seal it.
8. Using a sharp, serrated bread knife, cut the roll ever 1 ½ inches to make approximately 12 swirl buns.
9. Place the rolls, swirl side up, in the prepared baking dish.
10. Cover the rolls loosely with a damp tea towel and let them rise until doubled in size. (about an hour)
11. Preheat oven to 350 degrees F.
12. Bake for 25-30 minutes. Let cool in the baking dish for 10 minutes.
13. Zest an orange into a bowl. Juice the orange into a separate bowl. Add 3 Tablespoons of the juice into the bowl with the zest and reserve the rest to thin the icing if need be.
14. Whisk together the zest and juice with the confectioners' sugar until smooth.
15. Spoon over the swirl buns and enjoy!

Variations:

▪ Use vanilla icing. Replace the orange juice with flax/soy milk, and omit the zest. Add ½ teaspoon pure vanilla extract.

Mocha Swirl Buns

Ingredients:

Buns:
1 batch Sweet Dough (page 66)
12 Tablespoons dairy-free margarine, softened slightly
1/3 cup granulated sugar
2 Tablespoons unsweetened cocoa powder
Icing:
1 ¼ cups confectioners' sugar
3 Tablespoons prepared and cooled coffee *
½ teaspoon pure vanilla extract

Directions:

1. Grease a 9x13 inch baking dish with dairy-free margarine or shortening.
2. Prepare the filling by whisking together the granulated sugar and cocoa powder in a bowl.
3. Roll out the dough into a 10x18 inch rectangle on a lightly floured surface.
4. Using a spatula or an offset spatula, spread the dairy-free margarine over the dough. Leave a 1 inch border along one of the long sides.
5. Sprinkle the margarine evenly with the cocoa powder and sugar.
6. Using your finger, brush the clean border edge with water.
7. Tightly roll the dough toward the clean border edge, and then pinch the seam to seal it.
8. Using a sharp, serrated bread knife, cut the roll every 1 ½ inches to make approximately 12 swirl buns.

9. Place the rolls, swirl side up, in the prepared baking dish.
10. Cover the rolls loosely with a damp tea towel and let them rise until doubled in size. (about an hour)
11. Preheat oven to 350 degrees F.
12. Bake for 25-30 minutes. Let cool in the baking dish for 10 minutes.
13. Whisk together the coffee and the confectioners' sugar until smooth.
14. Spoon over the swirl buns, let the icing set for about 10 minutes, set, and enjoy!

Variations:

- Use vanilla icing for a chocolate vanilla swirl bun! Replace coffee with flax milk.

I always use instant decaf so I can make just one small cup quickly, and be able to serve these swirl buns to my children. Use any coffee you have on hand!

Blueberry Lemon Twists

Ingredients:

Buns:
1 batch Sweet Dough (page 66)
11 oz. Blueberries
¼ cup granulated sugar
¼ cup water
3 Tablespoons water +1 ½ Tablespoons cornstarch
Icing:
1 ¼ cups confectioners' sugar
3 Tablespoons flax/soy milk
½ teaspoon fresh lemon juice
Zest of one lemon

Directions:

1. Prepare two baking sheets by lining them with parchment paper.
2. Prepare the filling by stirring together the blueberries, sugar, and ¼ cup water in a saucepan over medium heat. Bring to a simmer, mash with a potato masher, and cook until slightly thickened.
3. Make a slurry by mixing together the 3 Tablespoons water and the cornstarch. Stir the slurry into the strawberry mixture and heat over low until thickened. Remove from heat and cool.
4. Roll out the dough into a 10x18 inch rectangle on a lightly floured surface.
5. Using a spatula or an offset spatula spread the strawberry mixture over the dough. Leave a 1 inch border on one of the long sides.

6. Using your finger, brush the clean border edge with water.
7. Tightly roll the dough toward the clean border edge, and then pinch the seam to seal it.
8. Using a sharp, serrated bread knife, cut the roll ever 1 ½ inches to make approximately 12 slices.
9. Using slightly damp fingers, gently flatten each of the slices into an oval. Twist each oval in the middle to form a figure 8 and place on a prepared baking sheet. (This step is very messy, but the finished product will be delicious!)
10. Cover the twists loosely with a damp tea towel and let them rise in a warm place for about 25 minutes.
11. Preheat oven to 350 degrees F.
12. Bake for 25-30 minutes. Let cool on the baking sheets for 3 minutes, then remove to a cooling rack to cool completely.
13. Whisk together confectioners' sugar, 3 Tablespoons flax milk, lemon zest, and lemon juice. Thin with more flax milk if need be.
14. Spoon over the twists, let dry, and enjoy!

Variations:

- Make Blueberry Lemon Swirl buns! Follow this twist recipe up to step number 8, then place the slices in a greased 9x13 baking dish, as you would for the Cinnamon Swirl Buns recipe. Let rise for an hour, and bake for 25-30 minutes. Spoon the icing over the top of cooled buns and enjoy!

Monkey Bread

Ingredients:
1 batch Sweet Dough (page 66)
1 cup granulated sugar
3 teaspoons cinnamon
1 cup dairy-free margarine
½ cup light brown sugar

Directions:
1. In a gallon zip top bag, mix the granulated sugar and the cinnamon.
2. Form the ball of sweet dough into a log, about 3 inches in diameter.
3. Using a chef's knife or a dough cutter, slice the log into 1 inch slices. Then, cut each slice into quarters to make "dough nuggets."
4. Place the dough nuggets into the zip top bag with the cinnamon sugar, seal, and shake to coat all sides of all the nuggets.
5. Place the nuggets evenly in a Bundt pan. And let rise for about an hour.
6. Preheat the oven to 350 degrees F.
7. Melt the margarine and brown sugar together in a small saucepan over medium-high heat. Stir for a few minutes until the mixture becomes uniform in color.
8. Pour the margarine/brown sugar mixture over the dough nuggets in the Bundt pan.
9. Bake for 35-40 minutes, or until the crust is dark brown.
10. Cool in the pan for 20 minutes before turning out onto a serving plate.

Twisted Chocolate Loaf

Ingredients:

Loaf:

1 batch Sweet Dough (page 66)

6 Tablespoons dairy-free margarine, at room temperature

1/3 cup oats

½ teaspoon imitation almond extract

½ cup granulated sugar

¼ cup dark cocoa powder

¼ cup unsweetened cocoa powder

2 teaspoons ground cinnamon

1/8 teaspoon ancho chili powder

3 Tablespoons vegetable oil, 3 Tablespoons water, ½
   Tablespoon aluminum free baking powder (Whisk
   together in a mug until frothy and add as one ingredient.
   This is your egg substitute.)

Topping:

¼ cup granulated sugar

½ teaspoon ground cinnamon

¼ cup dairy-free margarine, melted

Directions:

1. Prepare a baking sheet by lining with parchment paper
2. In a food processor, combine the room temperature
   dairy-free margarine, oats, imitation almond extract,
   granulated sugar, cocoa powders, cinnamon, ancho chili
   powder, and egg substitute. Pulse to make a paste.
   Make sure ingredients are evenly incorporated.
3. Roll out the dough into a 10x18 inch rectangle on a
   lightly floured surface.

4. Using a spatula or an offset spatula spread the cocoa paste over the dough. Leave a 1 inch border along one of the long sides.
5. Using your finger, brush the clean border edge with water.
6. Tightly roll the dough toward the clean border edge, and then pinch the seam to seal it.
7. Place the roll seam-side down on the prepared baking sheet. Refrigerate for about 30 minutes to firm up the roll.
8. Slide the parchment, with the roll on it, off the baking sheet.
9. Cut the log in half, lengthwise, using a sharp, serrated bread knife. Use gentle, careful strokes, to work your way down through the layers. You should see alternating stripes of dough and filling on the open face of each half.
10. Pinch one of the ends together with the cut edges facing slightly inward. Then, cross the right half over the left while you gently guide the left under the right. , and continue that pattern, straightening the loaf as you go.
11. Pinch the ends together to seal the loaf. Your loaf should have a beautiful twisted pattern of visible layers.
12. Cover the loaf with a damp tea towel and let it rise in a warm place for 30 minutes.
13. Preheat oven to 350 degrees F.
14. Remove the tea towel and bake the loaf for 30 – 35 minutes, or until golden brown. (To ensure even cooking, rotate the baking sheet halfway through.)
15. Slide the parchment and loaf onto a cooling rack.

16. To make the topping, stir together the cinnamon and sugar in a bowl. In a separate bowl, melt the dairy-free margarine.
17. Using a pastry/basting brush, brush the loaf with the melted margarine and then sprinkle with most of the cinnamon sugar. After the loaf is completely cooled, sprinkle with the remaining sugar and enjoy!

Cakes

5 Minute Cake in a Cup

This is the perfect quick treat for spur of the moment mini-celebration, for rainy days, for late night nibbles, or for any other time you just really need some chocolate cake, fast!

Ingredients:
1 large (mocha style) coffee mug
¼ cup unbleached all-purpose flour
¼ cup (heaping) granulated sugar
2 Tablespoons dark cocoa powder
Dash of kosher salt
3 Tablespoons canola oil
3 Tablespoons vanilla flavored flax/soy milk
¼ teaspoon pure vanilla extract
2 Tablespoons water mixed with 1 ½ teaspoon powdered egg-replacer
confectioners' sugar for dusting

Directions:
1. Whisk dry ingredients together in the mug until uniform in color
2. Add the wet ingredients and whisk everything together until smooth.
3. Microwave on high for 2 minutes and 20 seconds.
4. Top with a sprinkle of confectioners' sugar and enjoy!

Variations:
- Double this recipe (mixing it in a large bowl) and divide the batter into 6-7 "tasting cups" for a perfect kid-sized sweet snack! Place all the tasting cups in the microwave at once and cook for approximately 4 minutes.

Chocolate Cake

Ingredients:
3 cups unbleached all-purpose flour
2 cups granulated sugar
¼ cup unsweetened cocoa powder
¼ cup dark cocoa powder
2 ½ teaspoons baking soda
1 teaspoon kosher salt
2 cups water
2/3 canola oil
2 ½ Tablespoons distilled white vinegar
3 teaspoons pure vanilla extract
½ cup dairy-free chocolate mini-morsels.

Directions:
1. Preheat oven to 350 degrees F.
2. Prepare two round 9 inch cake pans, grease and flour.
3. In a large mixing bowl, whisk together flour, sugar, cocoa powders, baking soda, and salt until uniform in color.
4. Make a well in the center of the dry mixture and add water, oil, vinegar, and vanilla. Whisk until the cake batter is smooth. Stir in chocolate mini-morsels.
5. Pour half the batter into each of the prepared pans and bake for 30 -35 minutes, or until a toothpick inserted into the center comes out clean.
6. Set pans on cooling racks for 10 minutes.
7. Turn cakes out onto the racks and cool completely before frosting.

Variations:

- Bake in a floured and greased 9x13 pan for 35-40 minutes.
- Make 24 cupcakes. Bake for 20 minutes.

The "At Last" Yellow Cake

I cannot tell you how many yellow cake failures we have had in our kitchen! There have been many, many recipes adjusted, readjusted, thrown out, and giggled about. Baking a decent yellow cake without eggs is a difficult task. Finally, I came up with this recipe, and "at last" we have a go-to yellow cake for birthdays or cupcakes for every occasion!

Ingredients:
2 cups unbleached all-purpose flour
2 ¼ teaspoons baking powder
¼ teaspoon salt
1 ¼ cups granulated sugar
½ cup vegetable shortening
1 cup vanilla flavored flax milk
6 Tablespoons vegetable oil, 6 Tablespoons water, 1 Tablespoon aluminum free baking powder (Whisk together in a mug until frothy and add as one ingredient. This is your egg substitute.)
1 teaspoon pure vanilla extract

Directions:
1. Preheat oven to 350 degrees F. Prepare two 9-inch round cake pans, grease and flour.
2. In an electric stand mixer fitted with the paddle attachment, cream together the shortening and the granulated sugar.
3. Add the egg substitute and vanilla extract, and mix thoroughly.

4. In a separate bowl, whisk together the flour, baking powder, and salt.
5. Measure out the flax milk.
6. Alternate adding 1/3 of the flour mixture and 1/3 of the flax milk, mixing thoroughly after each addition, until all the ingredients are incorporated fully.
7. Divide batter equally between the two cake pans and bake for 30-35 minutes, or until a toothpick inserted into the center comes out clean.
8. Let cool in pans for 10 minutes before gently turning out onto cooling racks. This cake is delicate, be very careful when flipping it over, use a cake round or a flat plate to assist!

Variations:
- Pour all the batter into a greased and floured 9x13 baking dish. Bake for 35-40 minutes.
- Line 24 cupcake tins with liners, fill each about 2/3 full. Bake for 20 minutes. Let cool completely before frosting.

Cake Balls

Cake balls are a fun spin on the traditional cake and frosting combination. These can be dressed down for kiddos, or dressed up for a fancy adult dinner party. The flavor combinations are limited only by your imagination! Some of our favorites are yellow cake with orange flavored frosting, yellow cake with mint flavored frosting, chocolate cake with raspberry flavored frosting, and chocolate cake with chocolate non-buttercream frosting.

Ingredients:
1 chocolate cake (page 82) or 1 yellow cake (page 84)
1 ½ cups decorating frosting, (page 96), flavored with
      your favorite extract
2 bags dairy-free chocolate morsels

Directions:
1. Crumble the baked cake layers into a large bowl. The biggest chunks should be no bigger that a half-dollar.
2. Add 1 ½ cups of decorating frosting and mix it all together with your hands until the frosting is completely incorporated. Your hands should be a sticky mess!
3. Using a 2 teaspoon cookie scoop to ensure evenly sized cake balls, roll cake balls and place on a baking sheet lined with waxed paper.
4. Melt chocolate morsels in the microwave, stirring at 30 second intervals.
5. Dip cake balls into melted chocolate to coat, and place back on waxed paper to set. These can be placed in the fridge until the chocolate hardens.
6. Serve and enjoy!

<u>Variations:</u>
- Sprinkle with colorful sprinkles, or with sparkly decorator sugars.
- Add a shot of flavored liquor to the cake and frosting mixture for "grown-up" cake balls.

Grandma Betty's Blueberry Grunt Cake

This generously sized grunt cake takes me right back to my childhood. The original recipe, as it was passed down to me, is loaded with eggs and butter, but I've managed to recreate the taste and goodness with my adjustments so that a family tradition can live on. My Grandma Betty made this for my mom when she was little, my mom made it for me, and now I make it for my own children. A love letter through the generations…

Ingredients:
Cake:
3 cups granulated sugar
1 cup shortening
¾ cup vegetable oil, ¾ cup water, 2 Tablespoons aluminum-
    free baking powder (Whisk together in a mug until frothy
    and add as one ingredient. This is your egg substitute.)
4 teaspoons pure vanilla extract
3 cups flax (or soy) milk
7 cups unbleached all-purpose flour
¾ cup aluminum-free baking powder
2 teaspoons salt
6 cups fresh blueberries dredged lightly in flour
½ cup granulated sugar (to sprinkle on the inner layer)
Topping:
½ cup granulated sugar
2 teaspoons ground cinnamon

Directions:

1. Preheat oven to 375 degrees F.
2. Prepare an 18x12 cake pan by greasing with shortening.
3. In an electric mixer fitted with a paddle attachment, cream together the shortening, sugar, egg substitute, and vanilla.
4. Add the flax milk and blend until just incorporated.
5. In a separate bowl, whisk together the flour, baking powder, and salt.
6. Slowly blend the dry ingredient mix into the wet mixture.
7. Spread half of the batter into the prepared pan and then sprinkle with ½ cup of granulated sugar.
8. Evenly spread the dredged blueberries on top of the layer of sugar.
9. Cover the blueberries carefully with the remaining cake batter.
10. Mix the cinnamon sugar topping in a small bowl and sprinkle over the top of the cake.
11. Bake for 45-55 minutes. The center of the cake should appear firm and should not jiggle.
12. Set the cake pan on a cooling rack and cool for 15 minutes. Serve warm.

Pumpkin Mini-Bundt Cakes

Ingredients:
Cake:
2 ¼ cups unbleached all-purpose flour
1 ½ cups granulated sugar
2 teaspoons aluminum - free baking powder
½ teaspoon salt
1 cup dairy-free margarine, at room temperature
6 Tablespoons vegetable oil, 6 Tablespoons water, 1 Tablespoon
     Aluminum - free baking powder (Whisk together in a mug
     until frothy and as one ingredient. This is your egg
     substitute.)
1 cup pumpkin puree, canned or fresh
1 teaspoon cinnamon
½ teaspoon ground ginger
½ teaspoon freshly ground nutmeg
1/8 teaspoon ground allspice
2 teaspoons pure vanilla extract
Glaze:
1 ¼ cups confectioners' sugar
3 ½ Tablespoons freshly squeezed orange juice
Zest of one orange (use a microplane to zest the orange)

Directions:
1. Preheat the oven to 350 degrees F.
2. Prepare two mini-Bundt trays by greasing and flouring
   well.

3. In an electric mixer, using the paddle attachment, mix together the flour, granulated sugar, baking powder, and salt on low speed.
4. Add the margarine and blend on low speed until the mixture looks like coarse crumbs.
5. In a separate bowl, whisk together the egg substitute, pumpkin, spices, and vanilla.
6. Slowly add the wet mixture to the dry while the mixer is on low speed until just incorporated. Increase the speed to medium-high and beat until fluffy, about 2 minutes.
7. Spoon the batter into a zip top bag, (or a piping bag). Snip the tip of the bag to create a ½ inch opening, and pipe the batter in to fill pans about 2/3 of the way up. Do not overfill!
8. Bake for 18 minutes or until golden brown on top.
9. Set trays on cooling racks for 5 minutes and then remove cakes to the cooling rack by flipping the pans over gently. Cool completely.
10. Make the glaze by whisking together the confectioners' sugar, orange juice, and orange zest.
11. Dip the tops of the mini-Bundt cakes in the glaze and set on the cooling rack to dry. (Place some parchment under the cooling racks to catch the drips!)

Frostings

Pourable Chocolate Frosting

This frosting is best for cakes that remain in the pan.

Ingredients:
1 ½ cups powdered sugar
1/3 cup water or Flax milk (or soy milk, coconut milk, etc.)
5 Tablespoons dairy-free margarine
10 oz. bag of dairy-free chocolate morsels
1 teaspoon pure vanilla extract

Directions:
1. In a saucepan, melt the water, powdered sugar, and margarine.
2. Bring mixture to a boil and boil for one minute.
3. Immediately remove from heat and stir in the morsels.
4. Once chocolate is completely melted, stir in vanilla extract.
5. Pour over cake immediately, this frosting sets fairly quickly! The end result, when the frosting is completely cooled, is a wonderfully thick ganache-like frosting.

Variations:
- Add other flavor extracts like orange, raspberry, or peppermint for a whole new experience!

Decorating Frosting

This frosting is perfect for piping decorations onto your cake. After decorating your cake, chill it in the fridge for an hour or two to set the frosting.

Ingredients:
1 cup vegetable shortening
1 cup dairy-free margarine
2 teaspoons pure vanilla extract
3 Tablespoons water
2 lbs. confectioners' sugar
1/8 teaspoon salt

Directions:
1. In an electric stand mixer* fitted with the whisk attachment, cream together the margarine and shortening.
2. Add the vanilla extract and water, blend well.
3. Add the confectioners' sugar in several batches until completely incorporated.
4. If frosting is too stiff to spread, add a teaspoon of water at a time to reach desired consistency.

Variations:
- Replace vanilla extract with your favorite extract flavor!

*A handheld electric mixer will also work great!

Chocolate "Non-buttercream" Frosting

This frosting is perfect for piping decorations onto your cake. After decorating your cake, chill it in the fridge for an hour or two to set the frosting.

Ingredients:

1 cup vegetable shortening
1 cup dairy-free margarine
2 teaspoons pure vanilla extract
4-5 Tablespoons water
¼ cup dark cocoa powder
½ cup unsweetened cocoa powder
2 lbs. confectioners' sugar
1/8 teaspoon salt

Directions:

1. In an electric stand mixer* fitted with the whisk attachment, cream together the margarine and shortening.
2. Add the vanilla extract and water, blend well.
3. Add cocoa powders and blend until just incorporated.
4. Add the confectioners' sugar in several batches until completely incorporated.
5. If frosting is too stiff to spread, add a teaspoon of water at a time to reach desired consistency.

Variations:

- Replace vanilla extract with orange or raspberry extract for a classy twist!

*A handheld electric mixer will also work great!

"Sunbutter" Frosting

Pair with chocolate cake as an awesome alternative way to achieve the chocolate/peanut butter combo that creates such decadent desserts!

Ingredients:
¾ cup vegetable shortening
1 cup dairy-free margarine
1 cup smooth sunflower seed spread
1 teaspoons pure vanilla extract
1 ½ teaspoons "Real Lemon" concentrate
5 Tablespoons water
2 lbs. confectioners' sugar
Pinch of salt

Directions:
1. In an electric stand mixer* fitted with the whisk attachment, cream together the sunbutter, margarine, and shortening.
2. Add the vanilla extract, lemon, and water, blend well.
3. Add the confectioners' sugar in several batches until completely incorporated.
4. If frosting is too stiff to spread, add a teaspoon of water at a time to reach desired consistency.

*A handheld electric mixer will also work.

Basic Sweet Glaze

Ingredients:

1 ¼ cups confectioners' sugar
3 Tablespoons flax/soy milk
½ teaspoon pure vanilla extract

Directions:

1. Whisk all ingredients together.
2. Drizzle over the top of baked good.
3. Let sit out uncovered and allow to dry.

Marshmallow Fondant

When I realized I would never be able to purchase an allergy-safe fancy cake for my children's birthdays, I took cake decorating classes so I could make my own. And then I learned, I couldn't locally purchase safe fondant to use for the classes either! So I learned how to make my own using marshmallows and confectioners' sugar. Clear your counters, wear short sleeves and put on an apron, this is hands-down, the messiest recipe in the book! But, the reward is worth it!

Ingredients:
1 16 oz. bag of mini-marshmallows
2 Tablespoons water
2 pounds confectioners' sugar
Vegetable shortening, to prevent sticking
2 teaspoons imitation (clear) vanilla extract (or any other clear extract flavoring you prefer.)

Directions:
1. Melt marshmallows along with 2 Tablespoons of water in a large bowl in the microwave, stirring with a non-stick spatula at 30 second intervals.
2. Measure out approximately ¾ of the confectioners' sugar and put it right on top of the marshmallow mixture in the bowl. Set to the side while you prepare the counter and your hands.
3. Using the shortening, spread a thick layer on the front and back of your hands, wrists, and about halfway up to your elbows. Get in between your fingers! (I know you think this is crazy, but trust me, the more thoroughly you grease, the better!)

4. Now, spread a thick layer of shortening on the counter, giving yourself enough surface space to knead.
5. Dump the marshmallow and confectioners' sugar mixture into the center of the shortening and begin kneading. (This is outrageously messy, just continue kneading and working the confectioners' sugar into the marshmallow, it WILL come together!)
6. Add the rest of the confectioners' sugar and knead the dough into a smooth ball. This will take about 10 minutes. *Re-grease your hands and counter if the dough starts sticking. Add a bit of water if the dough is cracking and not becoming smooth and elastic.
7. Coat the fondant ball with a layer of shortening, and then wrap with plastic wrap. Place wrapped fondant in a zip top bag and refrigerate overnight. You may store it in the fridge, wrapped like this for up to a month!
8. When you want to use the fondant, remove the bag from the fridge and let it sit out in the bag until it is room temperature and easily pliable.

At this point you can add food coloring, roll it out, cut it, and decorate!

Brownies, Candy, and More!

No Bake "Sunbutter" Bars

Ingredients:

1 ½ cups dairy-free margarine, melted
3 cups finely ground graham cracker crumbs
3 cups confectioners' sugar
1 ¾ cups + 2 Tablespoons sunflower seed spread
2 ¼ cups dairy-free chocolate morsels
1 teaspoon pure vanilla extract

Directions:

1. In a medium bowl, mix together the melted margarine, graham cracker crumbs, confectioners' sugar, 1 cup Sunbutter, and vanilla until well blended.
2. Press evenly and firmly into the bottom of an ungreased 9x13inch pan.
3. Combine the chocolate morsels with the remaining Sunbutter in a glass bowl. Heat in the microwave, stirring every 30 seconds, until smooth.
4. Spread over the graham cracker layer in the pan.
5. Refrigerate at least one hour before cutting into 2 inch squares.

Variations:

- Line mini-muffin tins with candy cup wrappers. Make a batch of the melted chocolate layer, and spoon a bit into the bottom of each candy cup. Roll the graham cracker mixture into small balls and place one in each candy cup. Make another batch of the melted chocolate layer, and spoon over each candy cup. Refrigerate until set, and enjoy your peanut-free "Sunbutter cups"!

Fudgy Brownies

Ingredients:

2 cups flour
2 cups granulated sugar
½ cup unsweetened cocoa powder
¼ cup special dark cocoa powder
1 teaspoon baking powder (aluminum free)
1 teaspoon salt
1 cup water
1 cup vegetable oil
1 ½ teaspoons pure vanilla extract
½ cup dairy-free chocolate morsels

Directions:

1. Preheat oven to 350 degrees F
2. Whisk together flour, sugar, cocoa powders, baking powder, salt until the dry mix is uniform in color.
3. With a spatula, stir in the water, oil, and vanilla extract.
4. Once ingredients are fully incorporated, stir in ½ cup morsels.
5. Spread mixture evenly into a 9x13 pan.
6. Bake for 25 to 30 minutes.
7. Let the brownies cool and "set" for at least 15 minutes before cutting into 2 inch squares.

<u>Variations:</u>

- Add 1 Tablespoon instant coffee granules when you add the liquid ingredients.
- Add 1 teaspoon orange extract, and only ½ tsp vanilla extract for orange chocolate brownies.

*Hint: In baking without eggs and dairy, it is extremely important to have accurate measurements. Be sure to use dry measuring cups for dry ingredients, and a liquid measuring cup for liquid ingredients. It can make all the difference!

"Sunbutter" Pretzel Balls

These little gems of goodness are creamy, crunchy, sweet, and salty. They are everything one could want in a dessert!

Ingredients:
2 cups of sunflower seed spread
2 Tablespoons dairy-free margarine
2 teaspoons pure vanilla extract
¼ teaspoon "Real Lemon" juice concentrate
2 cups confectioners' sugar
2 cups broken pretzel pieces
2-3 bags of dairy-free chocolate morsels

Directions:
1. In an electric mixer on medium speed, cream together the sunbutter, dairy-free margarine, vanilla, and lemon juice.
2. Add confectioners' sugar and mix until completely incorporated.
3. Smash pretzels in a zip top bag and mix into dough. You may have to knead the pretzels into the dough by hand to get them evenly incorporated.
4. Cover dough in the mixing bowl with saran wrap, and chill for ½ hour.
5. Prepare a baking sheet with waxed paper.
6. Roll the dough into bite-sized balls, and place them on the waxed paper. Return to the fridge, uncovered for another hour.
7. Melt a bag of the chocolate morsels over a double boiler, (or in the microwave on 30 second intervals).
8. Dip the balls to coat completely and return to the waxed paper.
9. Chill in the refrigerator until chocolate is set.

Variation:

- Leave the pretzels out for smooth and creamy sunbutter balls!

I store these in an airtight container, between layers of waxed paper, in the fridge to prevent them from getting too soft.

Dairy Free Chocolate Fudge

This is one of my most requested dessert items! I've made countless batches for our family, for bake sales, for edible gifts, for "Mom's Night Out" events, and for many, many holidays. Because there are so many possible variations, this fudge never gets that "same-old, same-old" feeling!

Ingredients:

2 cups dairy-free chocolate morsels
2-1/4 cups granulated sugar
1-3/4 cups "safe" mini marshmallows
¾ cup flax/soy milk
1/4 cup dairy-free margarine
1 teaspoon pure vanilla extract

Directions:

1. Line an 8-inch square pan with foil, extending it over the edges of the pan. Measure the chocolate chips into a medium heat-safe bowl.
2. Combine the sugar, marshmallows, flax/soy milk, and margarine in a saucepan. Cook over medium heat, stirring constantly, until the mixture boils.
3. Cook an additional 5 minutes.
4. Remove from heat and add the vanilla extract.
5. Immediately pour marshmallow mixture into the bowl with the chocolate chips. Stir until the chocolate chips are melted and mixture is smooth. Immediately pour into the prepared pan.
6. Cool in the refrigerator until it is completely cooled, about 1 hour. Remove from the pan and place on a cutting board.

7. Remove the foil. Cut into 1-1/2 inch squares. Store in an air tight container. Makes about 3 dozen pieces.

Variations:

- Measure ½ cup Sunbutter into heat-safe bowl with 1 ½ cup of chocolate morsels to make Sunbutter-Chocolate fudge.
- Add 1 teaspoon cinnamon and ¼ teaspoon Ancho chili powder for Mexican fudge.
- Sprinkle crushed graham crackers and mini marshmallows on top for S'mores fudge.
- Replace vanilla with orange extract, or mint, or raspberry.
- Sprinkle crushed pretzels on top for a salty and sweet fudge.
- Press crushed Oreos on the top of the fudge before it sets for cookies and cream.

Sponge Candy

We have had some wild and crazy test batches of sponge candy! This is a fun one for the kids to watch, when you add in the baking soda, it's very dramatic. The result is sweet, crispy candy that's as light as air. This makes a great edible gift!

Ingredients:
1 ½ cup sugar
1 ½ cup dark corn syrup
1 ½ Tablespoons distilled white vinegar
3 Tablespoons baking soda
1 teaspoon pure vanilla extract
24 ounces dairy-free chocolate morsels
Dairy-free margarine for coating the pan
*candy thermometer
*waxed paper

Directions:
1. Coat the bottom and sides of a 9x13 baking dish/pan with dairy-free margarine.
2. Measure the baking soda into a small prep bowl and set aside.
3. Combine sugar, syrup, and vinegar in a heavy bottomed stock pot over medium heat.
4. Stir until the sugar dissolves and then STOP stirring. Cook until the temperature reaches 300 degrees F.
5. Remove from heat and immediately stir in the baking soda and vanilla. MIX THOROUGHLY.
6. Pour mixture into the prepared dish and allow it to naturally spread.

7. Set the baking dish on a cooling rack and let it cool completely.
8. Break into pieces, or use a sharp serrated knife to cut into pieces. (A good bread knife works really well for this step.)
9. Melt the chocolate in the microwave in 30 second intervals.
10. Dip the pieces in the chocolate and let dry on waxed paper.

Variations:

- Add 1 teaspoon of orange extract to make the Buffalo favorite: Orange Chocolate Sponge Candy!

Hint: Humidity can affect this recipe. It is best to make during cool, dry weather!

Movie Night Caramel Corn

Make this caramel corn the day before, or early in the day that you'd like to serve it, it does require a little drying time. Enjoy for a family movie night, or for a movie "date-night-in" with your sweetheart!

Ingredients:
1 cup popcorn kernels
1cup light brown sugar
2 cups sugar
1 ½ teaspoon pure vanilla extract
3 Tablespoons dairy-free margarine
1 ½ teaspoon baking soda
1 Tablespoon kosher salt
water

Directions:
1. Prepare two rimmed baking sheets by lining them with parchment paper.
2. Preheat oven to 260 degrees F.
3. Pop your popcorn! We prefer an air popper. Then, place it in a big (clean) pot, or a LARGE bowl; you'll need to really be able to stir the popcorn without it spilling out.
4. Measure out vanilla extract and baking soda into separate prep bowls. (Trust me, you won't have time to measure it out when you need to add it.)
5. In a stock pot, combine margarine, brown sugar, sugar, salt, and 2 cups of water. Stir until the sugar is underwater.

6. Heat the mixture, without stirring, until sugar is dissolved and the entire surface of the mixture is bubbling.
7. Once it is bubbling, heat for 1minute and then remove from heat. Immediately whisk in vanilla and baking soda. The baking soda will make the candy mixture foam and froth and POOF!
8. Gently pour the mixture over the popcorn, stirring with a non-stick spatula, and coating the popcorn.
9. Spread the popcorn over the two baking sheets and place in the preheated oven.
10. STIR EVERY 15 MINUTES FOR AN HOUR! (Or until the popcorn looks dark gold.) If you don't stir, the bottom WILL burn.
11. Remove the pans from the oven and allow to cool completely. Then, break into chunks and serve!

Variations:

- After popcorn is cooled, while the popcorn is still on the baking sheets, melt ½ cup dairy-free chocolate morsels with ¼ Tablespoon vegetable shortening and drizzle over the popcorn. Allow the chocolate to harden and set before breaking the caramel corn into chunks!

Hint: There may be extra caramel coating left in the pot, be careful not to overcoat the popcorn.

Perfect Peppermint Patties

I LOVE peppermint patties, but alas, the versions at the grocery store all contain egg whites. Of course, I took on the challenge so I could share my favorite candy with my children. I fell in love with these beauties the first time I made them, and they still make my heart go pitter-patter and my mouth water! This recipe yields between 90 and 100 patties. These make wonderful seasonal gifts! (The recipe can be halved to yield a smaller batch, but really, why would you want to!)

Ingredients:
2 Tablespoons light corn syrup
2 teaspoons fresh lemon juice
5 Tablespoons and 1/2 teaspoon water
2 teaspoons peppermint extract
2 pounds confectioners' sugar
2 Tablespoons shortening
36 oz. dairy-free chocolate morsels

Directions:
1. Using an electric mixer with the dough hook attachment, stir together the water, corn syrup, lemon juice, and peppermint extract.
2. Gently add half of the confectioners' sugar.
3. Add shortening and beat on medium speed.
4. Slowly add the remaining confectioners' sugar until well combined.
5. Remove the dough from the mixing bowl and knead into a ball on a clean counter. If the dough is still too

stiff, add ½ teaspoon of water to make it workable. Divide the ball into two equal parts.

6. Take one ball and place on a sheet of waxed paper. Flatten slightly with your hand and then place another sheet of waxed paper on top. You can use a plate to flatten the ball a bit, and then use a rolling pin to work into a circle about 9 inches in diameter and 1/4 inch thick. Repeat for other ball.

7. Place each circle (still in the waxed paper) flat on a cookie sheet. Freeze until firm, about 15 minutes.

8. Place the frozen disks on a cutting surface and remove the top waxed paper. Using a small circle cutter (ours was about 1 1/4 inches), cut out circles and place them on a parchment lined cookie sheet.

9. Gather the scraps, roll into another ball, flatten and repeat until it's all used up!

10. Freeze for about 10 minutes. Meanwhile, melt the chocolate morsels. You could use a double boiler, but frankly, we just melt ours in 45 second intervals in the microwave!

11. Coat the patties one at time using a fork to dip, flip and drain off the excess. (This works much better if the patties are really good and frozen! Once they start to thaw out, they don't cooperate as nicely!)

12. Harden the finished patties in the refrigerator for AT LEAST an hour!

13. Store them in an airtight container in the fridge, layered between sheets of waxed paper for up to a month!

Fruit Filled Oatmeal Bars

Ingredients:
1 ¾ sticks dairy-free margarine
1 ½ cups unbleached all-purpose flour
1 ½ cups oats
1 cup packed light brown sugar
1 teaspoon baking powder
½ teaspoon salt
12 ounce jar of fruit preserves, any flavor you like

Directions:
1. Preheat oven to 350 degrees F. Grease a 9x13 inch baking dish with margarine.
2. Using the paddle attachment in a stand mixer, mix together the margarine, flour, oats, brown sugar, baking powder, and salt.
3. Press ½ of the mixture into the bottom of the greased baking dish.
4. Spread the entire jar of preserves on the layer of oat mixture.
5. Sprinkle the other half of the oat mixture over the top of the preserves and press lightly.
6. Bake until the top is light brown, about 30 to 40 minutes.
7. Let cool completely and cut into squares.

Variations:

- For a splurge, spread a layer of sunflower seed spread, and a layer of mini, dairy-free chocolate morsels in between the layers of oatmeal mixture.

Chocolate Dipped Pretzel Rods

Get the kids in the kitchen with you and let them help with this simple recipe. They will love to dip and decorate!

Ingredients:

1 bag of egg-free, dairy-free pretzel rods
2 bags of dairy-free chocolate morsels
½ Tablespoon vegetable shortening
Colored sprinkles (optional)*

Directions:

1. Line a baking sheet with waxed paper.
2. Melt together one bag of mini chips and 1/2 Tablespoon shortening in the microwave, stopping to stir at 30 second intervals. (If you want to get fancy, go ahead and use a double boiler for this step.)
3. Once the chocolate is melted, dip the pretzel rods in about halfway, spoon chocolate over the rod, and then let the excess chocolate drip back into the bowl.
4. Lay the pretzel rod on the cookie sheet and decorate with colored sprinkles.
5. Once the cookie sheet is full, harden the chocolate in the refrigerator for about an hour!

If you are concerned about artificial food coloring in the sprinkles, you can purchase naturally colored sprinkles in the organic aisle at your grocery store, or eliminate the sprinkles all together.

Chocolate Freezer Candies

These candies are so incredibly simple, and such an elegant addition to any cookie or dessert platter. They're also great on their own any time you need to satisfy a craving for chocolate. (I recommend using high quality dairy-free chocolate, such as Enjoy Life Chocolate mini-morsels.)

Ingredients:
Chocolate mini-morsels (one bag per batch of candy)
Add-ins: crisped rice cereal, raisins, dried cranberries,
      dried blueberries, broken up graham cracker cereal,
      chopped shortbread cookies, chopped Oreo cookies

Please read the labels on your local products to ensure that they are safe for your food allergic loved one.

Directions:
1. Line mini-muffin tins with gold foil candy cups.
2. Using only one bag at a time, melt morsels in the microwave, stirring at 30 second intervals.
3. Stir in an add-in. Add only ½ cup to start and then increase the amount if needed until you have reached your desired consistency. EVERY bit of your add-in should be GENEROUSLY coated in a thick layer of melted chocolate.
4. Using a 2 teaspoon cookie scoop, scoop the mixture into the candy cups.
5. Place mini-muffin trays in the freezer until candy is set.

Marshmallow Dippers

A special treat for cold weather! Kids love to swirl these dippers into their hot cocoa.

Ingredients:
Dairy-free chocolate mini-morsels
White nonpareil sprinkles
Red, straight, drinking straws

Directions:
1. Stick straws into marshmallows.
2. Melt morsels in the microwave, stirring at 30 second intervals.
3. Dip the marshmallows ¾ of the way into the chocolate and set on waxed paper so the straw is sticking straight up.
4. Dip the chocolate covered bottom part of the marshmallows into the sprinkles before the chocolate is set completely.
5. Let the chocolate set, and then serve with dairy-free hot cocoa*!

*Use the chocolate syrup on page 132 with flax or soy milk to make dairy-free hot cocoa.

Van Horn Sunday Pancakes

Almost every Sunday, after church, we indulge in pancakes or waffles. We've concocted many different variations over the years, and this is the base recipe that we start with. I store the leftovers in between sheets of waxed paper, in zip-top storage bags in the freezer. They reheat wonderfully in the toaster and allow me to give the kids a hot breakfast during the week, with very little fuss! This recipe will make between 40-50, 4 inch pancakes.

Ingredients:
6 cups unbleached all-purpose flour
Heaping ½ cup granulated sugar
¼ cup baking powder
2 1/3 cup flax milk
1 Tablespoon + 1 teaspoon pure vanilla extract
1 cup Seltzer water
1 cup water
½ cup + 2 Tablespoons vegetable oil, ½ cup + 2
        Tablespoons water, 2 Tablespoons aluminum-free
        baking powder (Mix this together in a large bowl and
        add as one ingredient. This is your egg substitute.)

Directions:
1. In a large mixing bowl, whisk together the flour, sugar, baking powder.
2. In a separate bowl, combine the Seltzer, water, flax milk, and vanilla. Make the egg substitute.

3. Add the wet ingredients and egg substitute to the dry ingredients and STIR (do not whisk) until fully incorporated. Do not over-mix, it will make your pancakes tough.
4. Add any "add-ins" at this time.
5. Using a 3 Tablespoon (size 20) cookie scoop, SCOOP batter onto a hot griddle, or a non-stick skillet. (Scooping will result in fluffier pancakes, but you may also pour the batter if you do not have a scoop.)

Variations:

- Add one bag of dairy-free chocolate morsels.
- Add your favorite fruit, to taste: blueberries, sliced strawberries, sliced bananas, grated apples with cinnamon.

Hint: Flip the pancakes when they begin to lose their shiny appearance.

Waffles

We love big, beautiful, square waffles for breakfast. Grab a Belgium Waffle Iron and get cooking! I store the leftover waffles in between sheets of waxed paper, in zip-top storage bags in the freezer. They reheat wonderfully in the toaster, so make these "big batch" waffles and enjoy all week long!

Ingredients:
9 cups unbleached all-purpose flour
¾ cup sugar
3 Tablespoons aluminum-free baking powder
4 cups flax milk
1 Tablespoon pure vanilla extract
2 ¼ cups water
1 cup Seltzer water
¾ cup water, ¾ cup vegetable oil, 3 Tablespoons
    aluminum-free baking powder (Mix this together in a
    large bowl and add as one ingredient. This is your egg
    substitute.)
dairy-free margarine for greasing the waffle iron

Directions:
1. In a very large mixing bowl, (we use a large soup pot), add ALL ingredients and whisk until just fully incorporated. Do not over-mix.
2. Melt the dairy-free margarine and use a basting brush to grease the waffle iron.
3. Follow manufacturer directions for timing the cooking of your waffles!

Carrot Pancakes

Ingredients:
*Full batch of Van Horn Sunday Pancakes (page 122)
1 Tablespoon ground cinnamon
¾ teaspoons salt
½ teaspoon freshly ground nutmeg
¼ teaspoon ground cloves
¼ teaspoon ground ginger
¾ cup light brown sugar
4 ½ teaspoons pure vanilla extract
6 cups finely grated carrot

Directions:
1. *Follow directions for Van Horn Sunday Pancakes, adding the cinnamon, salt, nutmeg, cloves, ginger, and sugar with the dry ingredients.
2. Add additional vanilla with the wet ingredients,
3. Add the carrot after the wet and dry ingredients are fully incorporated.
4. Using a 3 Tablespoon (size 20) cookie scoop, SCOOP batter onto a hot griddle, or a non-stick skillet. (Scooping will result in fluffier pancakes, but you may also pour the batter if you do not have a scoop.)

Variations:
- Add one bag of dairy-free chocolate morsels.
- Add your favorite fruit, to taste: blueberries, sliced strawberries, sliced bananas.

Simple Breakfast Syrup

Ingredients:
2 cups light brown sugar
1/8 teaspoon kosher salt
1 ¼ cups water

Directions:
1. In a medium saucepan, combine the brown sugar, salt, and water.
2. Stirring continuously until the sugar is dissolved, bring to a simmer.
3. Simmer for 20 minutes, uncovered, or until slightly thickened.
4. Cool and serve over pancakes or waffles.

Vanilla Honey Spread

Ingredients:
1 cup softened dairy-free margarine
4 Tablespoons honey
2 Tablespoons confectioners' sugar
1 vanilla bean

Directions:
1. Slice open the vanilla bean lengthwise and scrape out the seeds from the pod.
2. Add the vanilla seeds to the remaining ingredients in a bowl and blend with a hand mixer until uniform in color and texture.
3. Spread into a medium ramekin and chill.
4. Serve over pancakes, waffles, muffins, breakfast breads.

Rock Star Recipes

This bonus section contains a few of my favorite easy recipes that will make you feel like a **Rock Star** in your own kitchen. Impress your family and friends with your amazing skills!

Homemade Applesauce

Ingredients:

6 pounds organic apples
1 cup water
3 Tablespoons sugar
¼ teaspoon salt

Directions:

1. Peel and quarter apples, trimming out the core.
2. Simmer, partially covered for 25 – 30 minutes.
3. Blend with an immersion blender.

Variations:

- Add cinnamon to taste, after blending.
- Make homemade <u>Pear-sauce</u> by replacing the apples with organic pears. This is also a wonderful treat for kids and babies who are eating first foods!

Chocolate Syrup

We love this syrup for making dairy-free hot cocoa, drizzling over chocolate chip pancakes for a special brunch, and stirring into cold vanilla flax milk for a lunchtime treat!

Ingredients:
1 ½ cups water
3 cups granulated sugar
2 Tablespoons light corn syrup
1 cup unsweetened cocoa powder
½ cup dark cocoa powder
1 Tablespoon pure vanilla extract
¼ kosher salt

Directions:
1. Combine water, sugar, and light corn syrup in a medium saucepan. Bring to a boil over medium heat.
2. Once the mixture boils, reduce heat to low and slowly whisk in both the cocoa powders until fully incorporated.
3. Cook for 5 more minutes on low heat, or until slightly thickened.
4. Remove from heat and stir in the vanilla and salt.
5. Cool completely and store in an airtight container in the fridge!

Pure Vanilla Extract

Pure vanilla extract can get to be pricey, so why not make your own? This is the easiest recipe you could imagine, it just takes a little patience...about 6 weeks' worth! Homemade pure vanilla extract is wonderful to use in your own kitchen, and packaged in beautiful glass bottle, it makes a perfect hostess gift for the holiday season.

Ingredients:
6 whole vanilla beans
16 ounces vodka
Glass jar with a tight fitting lid (mason jar, glass bottle with a rubberized stopper)

Directions:
1. Split the vanilla beans lengthwise, place them in the jar.
2. Pour 16 ounces of vodka over the beans and close the jar. (Make sure the beans are completely covered with vodka.)
3. Let it sit at room temperature for 6 weeks. Give it a little shake every once in a while.
4. Use in all recipes that require vanilla extract!

Other Notes:
- Use cheap vodka. This will ensure that no additional flavors with compete with the vanilla flavor.
- Bourbon can also be used in place of vodka.
- You can top off the bottle after you use some to replenish your extract. Give it a little shake to mix it well.
- Lasts indefinitely!

Pumpkin Pie Spice

Ingredients:
8 tablespoons Ground Cinnamon
4 tablespoons Ground Ginger
3 Tablespoons + 2 teaspoons Ground Nutmeg
2 teaspoons Allspice
2 teaspoons Ground Cloves

Apple Pie Spice
Ingredients:
5 Tablespoons + 1 teaspoon ground cinnamon
3 Tablespoons + 2 teaspoons ground nutmeg
4 teaspoons ground cardamom

Directions:
1. Make these mixes and store in airtight containers to keep on hand for baked goods!

Index

Alphabetical by recipe name:

For more recipes and cooking tips, visit

www.theallergysafekitchen.com

17759341R00079

Printed in Great Britain
by Amazon